Dear Freind,

Thank you for your continued support and ~~incr~~...
Your eagerness to ...
inspiring

May Hashem {
of all your heart

MW01075522

שבת

~~nuoo~~ Lavrie and Shraga
Summer 2024/5784

the lawyer
and the mystic

The Lawyer and the Mystic

Published and Copyrighted © 2017
by
Simcha Press

Orders:
291 Kingston Avenue / Brooklyn, New York 11213
(718) 778-0226 / Fax: (718) 778-4148
www.kehot.com

ISBN 978-0-8266-0831-4

Printed in the United States of America

the lawyer
and
the mystic

Robert Kremnizer

SIMCHA
PRESS

Table of Contents

Foreword

The Mystic in this book is a completely fictitious character. He articulates the teachings of the Rebbes of Chabad, especially those of the Lubavitcher Rebbe, Rabbi Menachem M. Schneerson, of righteous memory. These teachings have been simplified and condensed so that those who don't have access to the original are able to benefit from the extraordinary wisdom contained therein. None of the wisdom in this book is that of the writer, and those few individuals who are already familiar with the material will recognize that this is so. The author is confident that those privileged people would want this learning published and shared with all people, no matter what their race, religion, or background.

Chapter 1

Jerry Aronstein lay in the hospital bed slowly becoming aware of his surroundings. He remembered that it was late in December and that much of the hospital staff was away celebrating their holidays. If the surgery he had just undergone had not been such an emergency, it would surely have been postponed for several weeks. Many of the hospital beds were empty; in fact, Jerry was all alone in a private room. Jerry slowly and gingerly began to inspect his body, to which all manner of tubes were attached. But every time he attempted to move, the pain was excruciating.

Suddenly, he heard his adult children excitedly observing that Daddy was awake, and, as he looked up, he saw the family crowding around his bed, looking down anxiously at him.

All Jerry could remember about the first day and night in the hospital was the constant stream of nurses and orderlies attending to various tasks, taking his temperature, monitoring his tubes, and bringing him meals that he had no stomach to eat.

It took a few more days for Jerry to be agile enough to deal with the few remaining tubes. The long periods of time in which he was alone gave him time to think.

Time to think in solitude is one of life's luxuries, assuming we have the capacity to do so. Many people, pushed and pulled by the rapid forces of daily existence, find little time to think. Most people, freed momentarily from the daily bustle, seek refuge in entertainment, sports, or other activities, none of which require much introspection. Jerry, on the other hand, having been trained in the secrets of mysticism, found the time precious and welcome.

Was he going to die? He was really not prepared for death. In his middle sixties, Jerry had taken a long time to learn how to live. This process of learning had been an extended and difficult one for Jerry because he was, like most people, totally unequipped with even the basic skills. It was only through many meetings with the Mystic, whom Jerry had learned to love dearly, that he slowly and at first clumsily began to learn the tools of how to live, as opposed to exist.

He had over many years learned to live a life focused on purpose and one which allowed him to begin realizing his full inner potential. To his initial amazement, Jerry found that this process of growth had nothing to do with the values held to be self-evident by general society. So it was that by the time he was shocked to see the blood on his pajama pants, Jerry's life had become ordered, balanced, and happy.

Children, grandchildren, and a wife he adored made Jerry a blessed man. He had sufficient money and, until he noticed the blood, apparent good health. Much more important, Jerry had learned to utilize his blessings which, as a by-product of learning his mission in life, fulfilled him totally.

It seemed like yesterday that Jerry was standing in the bathroom, holding the slightly pink-stained pajama pants, which he instinctively thrust behind him as his wife had entered unexpectedly. Acceding to her demands to see what it was that was troubling him, the sight of the blood resulted in an immediate appointment with a general practitioner, following which was an almost as speedy appointment to have a colonoscopy. The GP was quick to reassure Jerry and Rafaela that the problem was probably nothing. This sudden bleeding could have been from a multitude of benign causes.

Accepting the reassurances at face value, Jerry was shocked when, awakening from the colonoscopy, he was slowly and carefully lectured by the gastroenterologist on why he was concerned about the growth he had discovered. Although there was sufficient reason to require pathology, there still was probably nothing to worry about. However, when the results of the biopsy came back one day later, there was reason for genuine concern. The tumor was indeed malignant, and Jerry would need an immediate operation to remove part of his colon. For the first time, Jerry felt real fear. The prospect of cancer was terrifying.

One of the things that Jerry sought to establish with almost no success was what would happen after the operation. The variables that the doctors proposed were too numerous for Jerry and his wife to focus on until after the operation had been performed and the results analyzed. All they could do was anxiously wait until that time.

The specialist who had just left Jerry had explained that the operated area had been successfully cleansed and part of the intestine removed. The critical question at this point was whether or not the cancer had entered the bloodstream. This would only be determined in a few days after a further set of tests had been conducted. Because of the holiday season, the results of the pathology would not be available for an additional five days.

Five days until he discovered whether he was going to live or die....

Chapter 2

Most people, not faced with the immediate prospect of death, simply avoid thinking about it. For most normal people, death remains a bogeyman somewhere in the back of their consciousness, to be accessed only in moments of danger. Apart from filling a person with dread, the thought of death remains remote and impersonal. Being forced by circumstance to consider death was therefore a totally new experience for Jerry. He had learned to live but not learned to die.

The Mystic had taught him the greatest secrets of the universe, but all of these were preparations for, and tools in, living. The business of dying was firmly pigeonholed in a box labeled "for other people."

As for living, Jerry clearly remembered the moment in his life some thirty years before, when he realized from the Mystic that there may be something more to life than he imagined.

The Mystic, Rabbi Kaye, had been introduced to Jerry in unusual circumstances. When Jerry and his wife Rafaela's first child was old enough to enter preschool, the only available opening nearby was in a Jewish school recommended to them by a close, equally nonreligious friend. To enroll their daughter, Jerry had gone to the office, which was part of the synagogue.

There, Jerry was to meet with the kind of strangely attired Jews that he had on occasion seen from afar. His first reaction was that he was in the wrong place and that he should leave as soon as he could without appearing rude. He was surprised to discover that these bearded gentlemen spoke perfectly fine English and that they seemed warm and friendly, and yes, they were willing to accept the Aronsteins' daughter.

What followed was a strangely convincing sales

talk on how Jerry's daughter should not be the only one in the family to understand her heritage, and how with a little effort, Jerry could become a role model for her. To assist Jerry and Rafaela in making that "little effort," another rabbi, one named Kaye, would be available to assist. Kaye was to aid Jerry in learning one or two basic tenets of religious thought sandwiched into some time that Jerry would grudgingly provide.

To this day, Jerry blushed when remembering how long he had kept the ever-patient Kaye in his elegant waiting room. He then had no idea that exposure to Kaye would open the greatest secrets of the universe and empower Jerry to be able to generate real happiness. As he lay in the hospital bed, the thought of his own lack of consideration made him blush all over again.

Chapter 3

For reasons he would not have been able to explain at the time, Jerry began to make time to see Kaye on a regular basis; this was long before Jerry knew Kaye to be a Mystic. At first, Kaye kept the conversation focused on Jerry and his outlook on life. Jerry's opinions were a mass of insecure contradictions, as were those of most young men of his age.

Jerry squirmed when in hindsight, he was reminded of how little he knew about Torah. He remembered how when he was sarcastically demonstrating what he naively thought was his wit, he challenged Kaye. He ridiculed how Kaye could subscribe "to what a rabble of men wrote in some

outdated book." He marveled with the same hindsight how patiently Kaye explained that the Torah
was given to Moses on Mount Sinai and how Jews
believed that every word was G-d given. Carefully,
he explained that a great responsibility came with
this gift, which is embodied in a series of 613 com-
mands called *mitzvot*. Furthermore, this Torah contained all the secrets of the universe. There was no
question, he told Jerry, not answered in this book.

Although he remained silent at the time, Jerry
remembered thinking, if only that were true. Little
did he know then how passionately he would de-
velop the thirst to understand all those secrets and
to be convinced that the statement was entirely
true.

It was one question, however, asked by Kaye
which began Jerry's real journey to climb life's
mountain.

Kaye was about to leave Jerry's office after one
of their conversations. He was standing with one
hand on the doorknob. It seemed at the time like
a casual remark, almost an afterthought. "By the
way, I forgot to ask you. Are you happy?"

Jerry Aronstein was then a thirty-year-old lawyer who had so far had a relatively easy lane in life. Born to parents who had sufficient means to educate him well, he had then gone on to university and studied law. He had been able to join a prestigious law firm, where he had done well and had rapidly become a partner. His new and beautiful young wife, Rafaela, and their first child completed his badges of success.

Since, in conversation, Jerry had made sure to mention these badges to Kaye, he was irritated at the question, showing as it did that Kaye had not been listening. When Jerry rearticulated his success in business, his wife and new child, his beautiful house, and his Jaguar, Kaye lamented his inattention and cheerfully disappeared down the corridor from Jerry's office.

It was not until, professing forgetfulness, Kaye had asked the question for the fourth time that it occurred to Jerry to think about it.

Chapter 4

Jerry's father had died when Jerry was in his early thirties, and Jerry had never really come to terms with whether his father's death was one of the great losses in his life or one of the greatest re-liefs.

Born in Poland in 1910, it seemed that Jerry's father had struggled through the first half of the twentieth century under the heel of anti-Semitism and was subjected to some of its cruelest man-ifestations both at school and then at university. Although he professed himself to be a proud Jew, Jerry really saw little evidence of this. His parents' friends were more or less equally distributed be-tween Jews and Gentiles, and most of the things that seemed to win the approval of his father were those achievements that conveyed status in the world around him: education, culture, and class, more than just money, were the accomplishments admired by Jerry's father.

As was fashionable at the time of his growing up, Jerry's father maintained a short, sleek haircut, mirror-shiny shoes, and knife-edged creases in suits as expensive as he could possibly afford, none of which masked the fact that he was short and corpulent. He was inflexible and strong, a man of principle, but lacking imagination. Jerry was an only child who adored his father but found his rigidity and demanding nature oppressive.

When Jerry began his series of lessons with the Mystic, Jerry's father made no effort to disguise his displeasure.

"We left all of that behind in the Holocaust when the Nazis butchered all our families," Jerry's father said, almost by way of an order. Until Jerry's father died, Jerry had no way of sorting out in his own mind who "we" were. Jerry's father felt free to issue edicts of this kind, and the mere fact that they were issued somehow or other forced Jerry to be included in them. It was not until well after his father had died that Jerry was able to begin to think in terms of an "I," distinct from the values and demands of his father and mother.

"Ask your holy man Kaye where G-d was in the Holocaust," Jerry's father once said scornfully to him as Jerry tried to share a piece of the Mystic's wisdom. Jerry actually did ask. It was way too soon, and Jerry didn't really have any appreciation of the depth of the answer.

"We don't ask G-d why," replied Kaye simply, "we ask, 'What can we *do*?'"

As always, efforts to relay any new insight failed as Jerry's father always waved away any comment as being irrelevant and unprovable, which in itself relieved Jerry of the burden of thinking any more deeply about it. The Holocaust would come up many times again with Kaye.

At his father's funeral, Jerry felt a sick feeling of disloyalty, grateful for the presence of Kaye immediately in front of him on the other side of the grave. Jerry would never forget the clods of earth hitting the box with their dull thuds. Lying in his hospital bed, he could hear those sounds as clearly as though they were yesterday's experience.

During the period of mourning prescribed under Jewish Law, which Jerry had decided to observe for reasons that he did not understand, Kaye was a constant and caring visitor.

On one visit, Jerry again repeated his father's question:

"Where was G-d during the Holocaust?"

The Mystic looked at Jerry with a saddened expression. Ignoring his previous answer about not asking but doing, Kaye replied, "The question is badly framed."

As Jerry lay in the grip of the tubes, he still remembered the Mystic's reframing of the question resounding like a rifle shot:

"The question is: Where was *man* during the Holocaust?"

Chapter 5

Long before the Mystic began to teach Jerry about happiness, he insisted on talking about responsibility. When asked questions by Kaye, Jerry always answered in a way that showed that he assumed his talents entitled him to certain superiorities.

"Why do you always compare yourself to other people?" asked Kaye one day as the two of them were sitting in Jerry's garden, which had taken the place of Jerry's office as their meeting point. Jerry had a large garden at the back of his house in which there flowered a huge avocado tree. Jerry and the Mystic would sit in cane chairs in the shade under the avocado tree whenever the time and weather allowed. This was already a year or two after Kaye had become available to Jerry.

When Jerry answered that life was about winning, whether in business, love, sports, or in any other form of endeavor, this obviously displeased Kaye, who remained silent for some time. Finally, Kaye interrupted the quiet sound of the rustling of the leaves in the breeze by saying:

"I need to tell you a couple of things about comparing yourself to others."

"Go ahead," said Jerry, immediately becoming guarded.

Ignoring the tone of defense, Kaye continued.

"Jews and Gentiles are different. Not better or worse, but different. Jews were created for a certain purpose and Gentiles for a certain purpose. A hand is not better than a foot, and a foot is not better than a hand. Both were created for their own special purpose as part of the body of humanity. A hand can certainly do a foot's job with difficulty and so can a foot do the work of a hand, also with difficulty. But both are more comfortable functioning true to their purpose.

"The same is true with Jews and Gentiles. Our

learning is that Gentiles were created to build the physical environment—and they have done, and are doing, a wondrous job. Architecture, theater, art, medicine, music, and the extraordinary advances in technology are just a few obvious examples.

"The mission of the Jews is to be a moral imperative in the world, breathing G-dliness into that physicality. This mission was given to the Jewish people on Mount Sinai and is embodied in the book written by G-d and dictated to Moses, mistakenly thought by you to have been written by a rabble."

Jerry moved uneasily, immediately quieted by Kaye's assurance that many Jews were just as ignorant of their heritage and it was nothing to be ashamed of.

"Jews, too," continued Kaye, "are doing a wondrous job. They have given the world monotheism and morality and function to make a dwelling place for G-d in the physical world.

"Within this dynamic, each person, Jew or Gentile, has a unique function with its unique challenges.

"More specifically, every person has a soul

which descends into a body for seventy, eighty, or 120 years on a mission and with a purpose. Gentiles are to work the physical, and Jews are to infuse that physical with the spiritual.

"Each individual soul will be given a body and an environment perfect for its mission. That environment will be specific: the time in which he lives, the place in which he lives, and, last but not least, the people that he meets and engages with. Each person then has the perfect equipment to accomplish the betterment of an environment specially chosen for him.

"Do you see then how irrelevant it is to compare one person with another?"

This being an entirely new way of looking at things, Jerry was not ready to show his excitement.

"I suppose so," said Jerry flatly.

Kaye paused, taking a sip of his black tea Rafaela had given him. After a moment or two, he continued.

"There was once a great saint called R. Zusha of Hanipol, who lived around two hundred years ago. This saint was a wonderful man but shockingly poor. There are many stories about him and his poverty, but one of the characteristics that he is remembered for is his constant joy, notwithstanding his physical surroundings.

"In common with other great Kabbalists, he knew the date on which he was going to die. Before his death, he was very sad. One of his followers, noticing this, questioned him, only to find out that R. Zusha was questioning his fate in the World to Come, but he was challenged that he must know how well he would do, so how could he be sad?"

Kaye looked at Jerry intently and continued.

"R. Zusha turned to his disciple and explained that he was crying because the question was not whether he had lived a good life for the disciple. The question was whether he had lived a good life for *Zusha.*

"In other words," explained Kaye, "the question that was causing the great man grief was whether he had lived out *his* potential, given *his* talents."

Kaye looked at his simple wristwatch and made a move to get up.

Jerry, looking at his expensive one, protested, "It is early yet; don't you usually stay an hour?"

"The above is a large mouthful," Kaye replied with a smile.

"I am still hungry."

Kaye chuckled and then continued.

"One of the biggest confusions in our society is talent and effort. We have reason to be proud of effort but not of talent. A person is born with talent. The amount of talent with which he is born is not his doing. What he *does* with that talent is his doing and something of which he can be proud. Conversely, if he does not utilize that talent to its full potential, he has what to be ashamed of.

"Comparing talents is worse than futile; it is stupid. Each person has his own task in his world and is given the talents to meet his own challenges. The question that you need to address, Jerry, is whether you are meeting your challenges with all of your talents or not.

"There is another and more sinister aspect to these comparisons. Most people allow themselves to be defined by other people's opinion of them. This is a deep mistake. To be a mirror for other people's opinions can be very unrewarding and destructive to self-esteem. A spiritually mature person determines how to live by learning sincerely and then putting that learning into action. His way of life then becomes deliberate. What relevance then is it what anyone else thinks? If someone laughs at you for putting on tefillin, since you worked hard to get to the point where tefillin are an integral part of what you do every day, who cares what the person laughing at you thinks? The only effect his opinion can have is to make you feel sorry for him and his ignorance. Allowing his ignorance to shape your opinion of yourself, or worse, to influence your action, is folly indeed."

Chapter 6

Jerry was awakened the morning after the surgery by the sound of the door to his hospital room being opened and then firmly closed again. Standing in front of him was the surgeon whose face Jerry had last seen immediately before the operation peering down at him in company of the anesthesiologist. The surgeon's name was Malcolm Thomson, and he looked more like a professional footballer than any form of doctor. Tall and straight with broad shoulders and neatly arranged, plentiful hair, he radiated total confidence and assurance.

After telling Jerry he had done very well, as though awarding a prize for good behavior,

Thomson went on to explain, in a kindly but detached manner, that he had managed to cut out what he believed was all of the problem. He was also able to do so fairly neatly, half by way of keyhole surgery and half by way of regular surgery. The results were very satisfactory, the only question being whether any of it had gotten into the bloodstream. Repeating what Jerry already knew, Thomson then told him that he would know about the results in another five days' time. Unfortunately, without the pathology, there was no certainty.

When Jerry inquired what would happen if the cancer had entered the bloodstream, Thomson replied that forty percent of people survived for two years....

What then? It was rare for Jerry to be left speechless, but there was no way he could sort out everything that was going through his mind at that moment. He simply stared at the surgeon. Sensing that the interview was over, Thompson announced that he would return when he had more information. He quickly left; he had other patients to see.

Chapter 7

Jerry could not understand why he continued to think about his father. He had been dead for over thirty years and had long since stopped being a frightening influence over his son. How he wished his father could have seen all four children grow up, thought Jerry. He would have liked the children, and the children would have liked him. Jerry was sure the kids would have dealt much better with his overbearing nature than Jerry had.

Although during his lifetime, Jerry's father seldom spoke of G-d or the Holocaust, picturing his face in the hospital room, Jerry was reminded of a dialogue with the Mystic.

"Once, in one of the death camps," said Kaye,

"the Nazi beasts decided to give the inmates a half day of leisure (though they always made the prisoners work especially hard on the Jewish holidays and Shabbat). There were three rabbinical judges also imprisoned in the camp, and somehow or other, it was resolved that the Jews would use the time to bring a court case against G-d. G-d was to be tried for inflicting pain, suffering, or, even worse, showing indifference. Arrangements were quickly completed. The case for the prosecution was to be stated by a great sage, and the case for the defense of G-d was to be argued by various people who reluctantly took the job. The matter was reasoned for some hours in the early afternoon, each side bolstering support from the Torah. When both sides had finished, the three judges considered their verdict in hushed tones. Total silence reigned in the camp when, accompanied by a bitter wind whistling through the wooden slats, came the verdict:

"'Guilty,'" announced the first judge.

"'Guilty,'" said the second judge.

"'Guilty,'" agreed the third judge.

"The silence was absolute.

"Suddenly, the head of the three judges stood

up and said firmly, 'It is now time to daven Minchah (pray the afternoon service)....'"

Jerry remained silent, considering the extraordinary apparent contradiction.

"This is how we live, Jerry," gently interrupted the Mystic, his strong but delicate face very serious. "We cannot explain many things, but that has nothing to do with our duty and our actions."

The paradox of the verdicts and the directive would have been totally lost on Jerry's father.

Jerry lay in bed reflecting on how much this paradox continued to trouble him. On another occasion when he brought up the Holocaust with Kaye, the Mystic said:

"It is not our job to be apologists for the Almighty. Our thoughts are not His thoughts, and we cannot understand any more than we can touch a musical sound with our hands. G-d doesn't need us to explain or justify Him, and I am not going to be His lawyer.

"On one hand, we argue with G-d about the Holocaust because we refuse to understand it; on the other hand, we continue our spiritual work.

"Having said that, let me sketch you an imaginary scenario. We will see together that a soul descends into a body in order to learn the Torah and to perform the commandments, so making a dwelling place for G-d in the physical world. There are 613 commandments, and a person needs to perform all of them that apply to him or her. What if he/she doesn't? We are taught that the soul splits off, the 'successful' part going to Gan Eden (Paradise) and the 'unsuccessful' part returning for another lifetime in another body."

"Keep going," said Jerry.

"Indeed," continued the Mystic.

"Now with that in mind, let me tell you that we have a tradition that if a Jew is killed *simply* because he is a Jew, he gets automatic entry to Gan Eden.

"So let me ask you a question. Suppose there were many souls that had tried and failed to perform all of the commandments, and they had run out of further lives for reasons beyond us, would it be for their benefit to die in the Holocaust?"

"I can't answer that," said Jerry.

"Still, all this is not our business. We are mystified because G-d can do anything, being all-powerful, and perhaps he could find a way to achieve His desired result in a way we could understand better.

"Now, Jerry," said Kaye with a wan smile, "let's go daven Minchah."

Chapter 8

Rafaela and the children had taken their turns helping Jerry try to eat his breakfast. They brought him his laptop and generally fussed around him in a way necessary for them to display their genuine love for their husband and daddy. Jerry was truthfully too uncomfortable to acknowledge more than a general sense of gratitude in having them with him.

One of the things Jerry had to do was to try to make real time to consider dying and to prepare for it. Yet, once his family had left the room, try as he might to think about dying, his thoughts slipped back to his sessions with the Mystic. He often focused on the early days when the words "By the way, I forgot to ask you. Are you happy?" reverberated around his consciousness repetitively but with no answer that satisfied him. Jerry's first reaction was to wonder what more could be had. What more was available to acquire? More money? More children? More pleasures? Amid the confused options, Jerry had then managed to reach one milestone. One thing he had concluded was that he wasn't unhappy, but was he happy? What did happiness mean? Jerry had never considered whether he was happy. How many young people, busily focused on getting through each day's problems, have the opportunity or luxury to consider whether they are happy? Wife, child, car, house—what else is there?

Jerry had instinctively felt that he wasn't unhappy, but then, he had no idea of whether he was happy because, come to think of it, he had no idea what happiness was. Was it pleasure? He had pleasure. Was it money? He had a measure of money. Was it a sense of well-being? Come to think of it, mused Jerry, he had never had a sense of well-being.

"I have a question to ask you," said Jerry at his next session with the Mystic.

"Ask away," Kaye replied with a smile.

"Are *you* happy?" asked Jerry, watching Kaye with intense concentration.

"Yes."

"What do you mean by happy?" Jerry continued.

"That is a difficult thing to tell you standing on one leg," said Kaye, "but it includes feelings of confidence, of total trust, of settled contentment, and of a positive knowledge of one's purpose and plans for the fulfillment of that purpose."

Jerry listened to this, stunned. He had never heard this language, and if he had, he had never heard it used in this configuration. Jerry realized that he simply had no idea what Kaye was talking about. The only thing he did know was that whatever it was that Kaye was talking about, he did not have it.

What confidence? Confidence in what? What trust? Purpose? Fulfillment? What had any of this to do with being cool and successful?

As if he were reading Jerry's mind, Kaye continued:

"Happiness is not a goal; it is a by-product. It comes from knowing who you are, what your mission in life is, and living consistently with this mission. I say to you, Jerry, with full respect and kindness, that I doubt you have any idea of this. You have no real sense of your core, you have no idea of your mission, and so, you have no chance to live true to that mission. This is not a criticism; it is a heartbreaking reality for most people."

Jerry's defense mechanisms springing into action were subdued by his fascination at what the Mystic was saying.

"Explain," asked Jerry softly.

"Your business is successful, you tell me. In order for this to be so, you have overviews of what you want to achieve. Presumably, you want to provide legal services at a profit. That is the reason your firm exists. That is the business plan, the mission statement, for your working. Your business plan isn't made up of the desks or the chairs or the furnishings or the technology. Those things are merely vehicles through which you want to achieve your business plan. You have no difficulty separating the furniture from what you need to do to make a profit.

"Consider, however, being born. We come with no directions. We come with no life plan. To have a successful life, we must *make* that plan. We will learn together what that plan should consist of, but for now, answering your question, when a person lives in accordance with that plan to better himself and his environment, his life has an entirely different dimension. Living consistently with, and growing the success of that plan, results, as a by-product, in happiness."

"How do you know what that mission statement is, or how to make it?"

"It is a process. It is a vital and wonderful process but a process nonetheless. We can't do it in one step. I promise you, when you know the four keys, you will get there yourself."

It had taken years for Jerry to find out. The answer lay in four keys which the Mystic withheld from him for years. Now that he knew them, Jerry understood why it necessarily took so long to learn.

Chapter 9

The feeling of violation when your home is burglarized is devastating. So it was that when Jerry and Rafaela had returned from a trip to Italy, the strangely disarranged furniture and comfort zones in their house alerted them immediately to the fact that they had been robbed.

Jerry and Rafaela had spent three romantic weeks abroad, the high point of which had been an extended stay at the Daniella Hotel on the main canal in Venice. The haunting silver light and the constant lapping of the waters of Venice soothed and stroked their relationship. The interlude was one both Jerry and Rafaela remembered as one of the most beautiful times of their lives. The dismay

and alarm that accompanied finding the house in-
terfered with was therefore like the bad aftertaste
of repeating food after a delicious meal.

After notifying the insurance company, Jerry
discovered that there would be a substantial loss
because of the way the company had calculat-
ed the value of their possessions. He shared with
the Mystic that he planned therefore to inflate the
value of everything stolen so that the insurance
company's unscrupulous valuation methodology
would be foiled and Jerry completely, if not justly,
compensated.

They were again under the avocado tree, with
the winter weather making Jerry shiver a little. He
noticed that, as usual, Kaye seemed impervious to
heat or cold.

"Do you remember I told you about a great
Mystic called R. Zusha?" asked Kaye.

"Sure," replied Jerry.

Kaye went on to explain. R. Zusha had a wife. It
is difficult to know who was greater, the great saint
R. Zusha or his worthy wife. Despite their poverty,
R. Zusha's wife provided the children with so much

spiritual warmth that the family flowered and grew into great saints themselves.

She once complained that for many years, she had not had the ability to buy a new dress. She begged him to put aside some money to enable her to have a new one sewn, and he complied. On Erev Shabbat, R. Zusha noticed that his wife was very thoughtful and subdued. "Why aren't you more cheerful?" he asked in amazement. "You already have your new dress; be happy." She told him that when she came to the tailor to pick up her new dress, she noticed that he was very sad. When she inquired why, he told her that his daughter was about to be married. Recently, the groom visited the tailor's home and noticed that he was sewing a new dress. The groom was under the impression that the dress was being sewn for his bride and was quite pleased. However, when he found out that it was not so, he became extremely upset. The tailor concluded, "Now I am afraid that because of his disappointment, the engagement will fall through, and my daughter will not marry."

"The tailor's dilemma moved me so much, that I told him to keep this dress as a present for his daughter, and thus, I am where I began. I still do not have a new dress." R. Zusha, after hearing his wife's story, had only one question to ask her. "Tell me, did you at least pay the tailor for his work?" His wife, in amazement, asked, "I do not understand you. Do you expect me to pay him when I gave him the dress to keep?" R. Zusha told his wife, "This is no excuse. The poor tailor worked an entire week to sew a dress for you, expecting to receive money to buy food for Shabbat. If you want to do a mitzvah and give your dress to his daughter, that is your business, but he deserves to be paid for his work." Following the instructions of her husband, she immediately paid the tailor.

With characteristic warmth when critical, the Mystic put his arm around Jerry and said, "You will remember, Jews have to be a moral imperative. Integrity, indeed, scrupulous honesty, is part of that imperative."

"I am only defending myself, though," said Jerry crisply.

"Understand that I am telling you this for another reason altogether.

"Curiously, although not immediately apparent, integrity is a condition of self-esteem.

"It is fascinating that lack of integrity is consistent with arrogance but not self-esteem. We will learn this later."

The Mystic left, no doubt being carefully punctual for whatever was his next activity.

Meanwhile, Jerry decided to postpone making the insurance claim for the present....

Chapter 10

Jerry was feeling markedly better. It was the afternoon several days after the operation. Sunlight was streaming through the window, and he was sitting up in bed watching birds hopping from branch to branch in the tree outside.

If the reality was that he had less than two years to live, Jerry wondered how he could prepare for dying. Obviously, there were all the practical issues of a will, money, arrangements, and so on, but there would be time for that. More importantly, there must be a focus on what he had learned with the Mystic all these years, which would help him. The problem was, thought Jerry, he had been taught how to live, but not how to die.

Jerry's mind drifted back to perhaps one of the most important sessions he ever had with Kaye. It is incredible how in life, some incidences stand out in stark relief, the details of which are so clear that you could almost reach out and touch the picture in your mind's eye.

It was in the afternoon under the avocado tree when Kaye finally told Jerry of the three blessings.

"It is a great secret of Kabbalah," explained Kaye, "that fundamentally, there are three blessings in a man's life.

"According to Kabbalah, three general blessings come to mankind and can only very superficially be controlled. These are: health (and therefore length of years), children, and money. Furthermore, very few people merit having all of these three blessings at one time. The incredible code in creation was, Jerry learned, that most people have at best only two of these blessings and sometimes only one, with some people none."

Jerry had now reached the level where he no longer automatically disagreed but questioned his lack of understanding. He wanted to know why there was no control on these blessings. Surely, if a man looked after his health, he would live longer. Surely, if he educated his children soundly, his children would give him pride. If he worked hard, he would be successful. It seemed to him that to a very large extent, there was truth in the saying that a person "makes" his own luck.

The Mystic assured him that this was only true at the most superficial of levels. Health was largely inherited. Of course, we have an obligation to look after our body and our health by diet, rest, and exercise. Nevertheless, a tall person cannot become short, and a person with poor health levels formulated by his DNA can only marginally improve his state of being. Similarly, with children, there were rebellious and unhappily unsuccessful children from the most scrupulous backgrounds. Indeed, even within one family, there are great differences in each child's makeup. As far as money was concerned, Kaye invited Jerry to consider how many people seemed to make and keep money with the most minimum of brains and talent, whereas others with enormous resources in that direction seemed to always be losing the battle to make ends meet.

"But why is that fair?" asked Jerry.

"Why is it that some people are so blessed and some people are so bereft? Aren't you saying that G-d is cruel, or worse, negligent?"

The Mystic became serious and thought for a moment before going on.

"It is too early to go into this in too much detail," said the Mystic slowly, but gathering momentum, he described that what came before and what came after is part of a Master Plan to which we are not privy. We all have a very limited ability to perceive and analyze our reality. In addition, our reality is very limited, and we are not aware of anything outside our perception.

"In reality, each man is the recipient of the exact blessings he needs. If his test is wealth, he will be rich; if his test is poverty, he will be poor. If his test is beauty, he will be beautiful, etc. In fact, life is a complex cocktail of situations suitable for bringing out the best in each person, who, in turn, has the best equipment to meet his particular challenges."

Kaye explained that the purpose of the conversation today was not to establish the truth of this. Jerry, he assured him, would come to recognize the truth of these blessings by observation during his life. There was a much more important question one relevant to Jerry immediately.

Kaye paused and looked at Jerry through narrowed eyes.

"The question is, is happiness related to having these blessings?"

Jerry took no time at all to answer.

"Of course," said Jerry.

"Are you sure?" asked Kaye.

"So if you have all three blessings you are happy, with two out of three you are two-thirds happy, with one of the three one-third happy, and with none suicidal?" Jerry sat listening in confusion. Before he was able to articulate what his knee-jerk reaction would have been, Kaye continued.

"We have all heard about famous people, entertainers, real estate magnates, people who have made billions in the stock market, who have committed suicide. They seemed to have every material blessing that a person could want. Why weren't they totally fulfilled and totally happy? With all they had, why were they so miserable that they had to commit suicide?" Jerry had no answer.

The Mystic leaned forward and put his glass of tea carefully on the table. He told Jerry that what he wanted to achieve with him that day was to begin to understand that happiness has very little to do with the quality or quantity of the very blessings that man in today's society supposed were so necessary.

"Then what does it have to do with?" asked Jerry, bewildered. He had always understood his life to be about money, family, and having a cool time with what it bought.

Instead of answering, Kaye asked Jerry whether he believed he was entitled to happiness.

"Of course," said Jerry.

"Of course?" asked the Mystic.

"Yes, of course," said Jerry firmly.

"How can this be?" asked Kaye. "If you tell me on one hand that your happiness is dependent on health, fine children, and plenty of money, then it must be that without them, you are going to be *un*happy. What you are really telling me now, and let's be clear, this is the general view of society, is that happiness is not a right but the result of some kind of huge supernal lottery. If you're lucky enough to be blessed with enough items, you are happy. If you are not, you are unhappy. Is that what you think? More importantly, are you satisfied with that? Are you content to live with that? How does this stand together with your insistence that you have a *right* to be happy?"

Jerry remembered the rabbi's intensity as he simply stopped to give Jerry enough time to consider this properly.

"You tell me happiness is a right, and if that is so, since the blessings don't come as a right, it must be that happiness can be *independent* of those blessings or the lack of them.

"You can learn, if you work at it, how to be happy independent of those blessings by accessing tools I will teach you. There are four keys to this, and we will learn them together."

However, Kaye assured Jerry, he was not ready for them yet.

Kaye started packing up his things and was deaf

to Jerry's pleas to stay and continue. He was insistent that Jerry spend some quality time carefully considering what they had learned.

 "What we have shared together today is more than enough to digest in one session," said Kaye. "We will talk more again. In the meantime, I want you to ponder whether you are prepared to make a commitment to be happy, irrespective of the fruitfulness of your efforts with health, children, and money. If I can see that you are really committed to that, we can then discuss how to go about it."

Jerry lay in his hospital bed, thinking about that afternoon years before. More than anything, he mused, straightening his blankets, that day and their next session changed his life.

Chapter 11

The next session began under the avocado tree as usual but later moved inside the house. Kaye began by asking whether he remembered what was said last week about happiness being possible independent of the blessings we receive and whether Jerry was serious about wanting to learn—and practice in his life—the tools to gain it.

"Of course," said Jerry.

"Then concentrate well as I am going to share one of the great life secrets of happiness with you. Although you are not ready yet for the four keys which are the tools for happiness, you have learned enough to understand this life secret, even if, as yet, you are unable to do it."

There was no criticism meant, and Jerry didn't feel slighted, having learned to trust Kaye's judgment, knowing by now that there was no separate agenda for the Mystic, simply the truth.

"Do you know who Joseph was?" Kaye began.

"Of course," said Jerry.

Kaye shot him a look that Jerry had by now learned was gently critical—usually generated by what Kaye saw as some level of conceit. Nevertheless, he continued.

"Our Patriarch Jacob had twelve sons, of whom Joseph was the favorite and the recipient of the well-known coat of many colors. He was sold into slavery by his brothers. Later, he became head of Potiphar's house but then was thrown into jail along with Pharaoh's butler and baker.

"Now, there is a verse in the Torah that is mind-boggling. It thunders and screams for understanding and when really understood unlocks the great secret I mentioned."

Kaye paused, looking keenly at Jerry to see whether his attention warranted the disclosure. Apparently satisfied, he continued.

"The verse is Joseph asking the butler and the baker why they were so miserable."

Kaye was silent for long enough for Jerry to start moving uncomfortably in his chair.

"So what?" asked Jerry sheepishly.

"Understand," continued Kaye gently and unfazed.

"There are two huge questions here; one is about Joseph asking after the other two and the other on why he was asking in the first place. "Let's begin with the first question," said Kaye.

"Here is a man who lost his mother at nine years of age and was sold into slavery by his very own brothers at seventeen. He was desired by his boss's wife, one of the most beautiful women in history. She relentlessly pursued him for a long time, yet he managed to withstand the temptation to violate the trust of his employer. What was his reward? He was thrown into jail—not any jail but an Egyptian jail. The only prospect there was pain, disease, and death.

"What do we see from this verse? His focus isn't on himself. He isn't blaming G-d, he isn't feeling sorry for himself, he isn't questioning his belief system. He is concerned about the butler and the baker!"

"Amazing," agreed Jerry.

"Now, what about *his* question? Is it a stupid question? What did he expect? The two men were locked up for life in a filthy, hopeless dungeon, and in this environment, Joseph is surprised they look miserable?!"

"Again, surprising," agreed Jerry.

"However," Kaye continued, "this would be a hasty and shallow conclusion. Joseph was super smart. He became the viceroy of Egypt, next to Pharaoh, the most powerful man on the planet. So we can't just say it is a stupid question."

"No," agreed Jerry, fascinated.

"Let's go inside," said Kaye.

Inside, Rafaela was feeding the baby in her high chair. The baby was smiling and gurgling while smacking the food on her plate with an open fist. Kaye pulled out a tiny toy car from his pocket and with a warm smile dangled it in front of the baby. The baby broke into squeals of delight as she tried to grasp the car. As Kaye was giving it to the baby, Rafaela vetoed the gift until after the baby had eaten. Obediently, Kaye withdrew the toy. Predictably, the baby's face fell, and delighted laughter turned first to surprise, then disappointment, and finally to woeful wailing.

Kaye hurriedly showed the baby he was giving the car to Rafaela, and both Kaye and Jerry hurried out to the safety of the study.

When they were seated, Kaye said:

"What happened in there?"

"What?" asked Jerry.

"What happened in there?"

"The baby cried."

"Why?" asked Kaye patiently.

"Because you took away the toy car."

"You are right, of course," said Kaye, "but consider this. There are really two ways happiness is elicited. One is *responsive*. You get something, you are happy. You don't, you are not. You get a new car, house, or toy, and your heart sings. You don't, and your heart feels disappointment and is heavy as lead. If your happiness is going to be tied to good things happening *to* you, your happiness in life will be dependent on those good things. Happiness in life is now a huge lottery. If things work out, you are happy, maybe. If not?"

"That's natural," said Jerry.

"Maybe so, but what happened to your saying you had a *right* to happiness? Here, there is no right, only luck."

"So what are you saying?" asked Jerry, confused.

"I am saying there is a second way to happiness that is not responsive. A child cannot do it. A child simply reacts. Perceived good, instant joy. Perceived bad, instant misery. A spiritually mature person is able to go beyond what is happening *to* him and put into context a bigger picture. It is too early for you to have these tools, but soon, you will reach a level where what happens *to* you can become almost totally discounted, replaced by happiness generated from *within* you. This will come from making and staying true to the mission statement we learned about. You will be able to do this with the four keys. The road to this is difficult and requires work and practice, and we will learn how together. But you, Jerry," he said, "like everyone, can learn it."

Jerry sat in silence, the enormity of what he was hearing quickening his heartbeat.

"How?"

Kaye smiled kindly.

"Slowly, we will learn it. Meanwhile, I will share a story of a Chasid interned in Siberia by the monster Stalin. He shared a bunk with three men, who were all successful and rich in Russia before their imprisonment. All three were seriously depressed. They became irritated at the Chasid's constant joyful good humor. One day, the men challenged him, demanding to know why he was always so idiotically cheerful. The Chasid in return wanted to know why his questioners were not. There was then an outpouring of bitter recrimination; one had been a brain surgeon, respected and prosperous. The second had been in charge of meat distribution and had made a fortune from the black market and lived like a maharaja. The third was a general in the army. People opened doors for him and fawned on him for favors. Here in Siberia, all three were cleaning latrines, prisoners respected by nobody. The Chasid sympathized and explained his situation was different because he had lost nothing by being in Siberia. In Moscow, he was a servant of G-d, meeting whatever challenges came his way, and here, he was a servant of G-d, meeting whatever challenges came his way. For the three men, happiness disappeared when their good fortune disappeared. Their whole perspective had changed. Their perspective was a product of what their external environment was. For the Chasid, his perspective was generated from *within* and totally consistent with his mission statement. His business plan was to serve G-d. Moscow or Siberia, hot or cold, nice furniture or no furniture, what was the difference? He used the four keys we will learn about, so for him, nothing had changed.

"Think deeply about this, Jerry. The tools for this we will learn together with the four keys. They involve understanding that G-d is in control and that control is for our good."

Monitoring the time, Kaye packed up to leave.

Jerry noticed Kaye slip the baby a second toy car as he made his way out, cheerfully calling goodbye to Rafaela.

Chapter 12

Rafaela and the children maintained their vigil at Jerry's bedside as he alternated between periods of wakefulness and somnolence. Considering how much time he was asleep during the day, it was no surprise that much of the night he was wide awake, giving him plenty of time to relive his sessions with the Mystic.

"Do you know what month this is?" Kaye once asked. "Of course; March," replied Jerry.

"I meant the Jewish month, and it is Adar," continued Kaye.

"I wonder if I can test you a little and ask *you* to explain some Torah to *me*."

Jerry hadn't come this far to believe he was going to get this right without help.

The Mystic smiled at Jerry affectionately and said, "There is a saying that when the month of Adar comes in, we must increase in *simchah*. *Simchah* is usually translated as 'joy' or 'happiness.' What do you think of that, Jerry?"

"Great," said Jerry, "what have you got planned?"

"No doubt we will party together," replied the Mystic, "but maybe I didn't make the question clear enough. How *do* you increase in *simchah*?"

Jerry knew better than to answer immediately and thought carefully.

"I suppose buy presents for the family, party, eat, drink, and be merry?"

Kaye smiled.

"All month?"

"OK. I give up. What then?"

"With our lessons so far, you can do better than that. If we need to be happier in this month, why can't we turn this around and say to G-d, 'You want me happier, give me more!' Give more money, better health, more *nachas* (joy and satisfaction) from the children. Give me more of all that, and I will be happier. How can you expect me to just be happier without any increased gratification?"

The light was dawning on Jerry. This is the point of the Joseph lesson, thought Jerry. This is what Kaye has been trying to get me to understand all along! "I guess the question is, who has control of the volume knob on one's *simchah*? Is that not the question?"

"*Yishar koach*!" thundered Kaye. "Tell me more."

"Well," said Jerry, thrilled by what was unfolding for him, "I suppose that is what we learned about real happiness not being responsive."

The Mystic, though calm, looked like he would burst with pride. Jerry proudly continued:

"The instruction to increase in *simchah* would be unfair and impossible if *simchah* was only responsive. If there is an obligation for more joy at a particular time, then we, those obligated, must be able to control it. I suppose therefore we have to say that volume knob on *simchah* lies with us."

"Exactly," Kaye replied, nodding.

"Still, obviously, everyone needs some level of blessing," said Jerry, not ready to give up the pipeline to good things happening to him.

"That goes without saying," said Kaye, "although for saints, no level is necessary as their happiness is generated totally from within, as we will learn with the four keys."

"So is that why Joseph asked the question?"

"Yes, as you said yourself."

"But the baker and the butler weren't saints?"

"The Torah is a blueprint for life, the wisdom of G-d written down. It is also the manual for life, and everything in it is a teaching. A butler and a baker can, with training and effort, reach the level of joy that transcends the vicissitudes of life, recognizing the challenges for what they are—gifts from G-d for our own benefit.

"If a butler and a baker can do it, even a lawyer has a chance," quipped Kaye, immensely proud of himself.

Chapter 13

Thomson, the surgeon, was again standing in front of Jerry at the foot of the bed. "You must walk," he said in his best professional manner.

Jerry remonstrated that he was wired up to a drip and, that being so, how could he possibly walk?

Thomson explained that the corridor outside Jerry's room formed up a large rectangle around the perimeter of the building and that he should make sure to walk that perimeter a few times a day. As far as the drip was concerned, he could wheel that next to him. When Thomson had again vanished, Jerry learned how to wheel the drip and began what became a series of regular walks during his remaining days in the hospital.

The walking brought to mind the first time Kaye had ever been late.

Rafaela had prepared tea under the avocado tree with a plate of biscuits of the kind that she always prepared, destined to remain untouched by Kaye. He ate very little and when they were together only sipped tea—a black tea bag in a glass. When Jerry had once questioned him about his austerities, Kaye waved his hand and said, "Leave that area alone for the time being and maybe forever. You should enjoy your ice cream and all else you like." He refused to comment any further, and whenever Jerry brought up the subject of his apparent lack of indulgence in anything physical, Kaye always insisted that the subject be changed to one where some positive action might result.

"Remember, Jerry," said Kaye with a warm smile, "action is the main thing."

He had frequently told Jerry that sighing alone would never do any good. It needed to be followed by resolve and positive action that would bring good into the world.

Jerry looked at his watch in concern. Kaye was never late. Twenty minutes late was uncharacteristic, and Jerry began to mull over the preciousness of the time being wasted for him. It took many years before Jerry learned that these feelings were inappropriate and came from unwarranted feelings of self-importance.

Meanwhile, once Kaye had arrived and had completed his apologies, he uncharacteristically did not sit down. "Would you mind if we walked a little, Jerry?" said Kaye.

"Sure," replied Jerry, "anything wrong?"

"I've been to the doctor, and he tells me that I must walk a little."

"Are you okay?" asked Jerry in alarm.

Jerry had never for a moment contemplated that he may be denied access to the Mystic.

"Yes, yes," said Kaye. He tapped his chest and said, "Not enough love in the heart."

"Is your heart OK, though?" said Jerry.

"Yes, yes, but I must walk," said Kaye.

"I'm into love," said Jerry absentmindedly as they walked from the garden to the street.

The Mystic sighed. "Are you sure, Jerry?"

"Of course," said Jerry, still at a sufficiently low level to think the Mystic had asked a silly question.

"I love what I do. I love Rafaela—I love our time together."

"Let us walk a little, and we will talk," said Kaye.

Kaye then began to gently tell Jerry that he actually shared society's confusion on what love is. Although the words that Kaye used formed sharp sentences, his tone and his manner was, as always, kind and embracing, taking the edge off any harshness whatsoever.

He proceeded to explain to Jerry that, for most people, love was a matter of self-gratification. Jerry's love was part of his perspective of acquisition. The things that Jerry loved were things Jerry believed he needed to fulfill him. In fact, explained Kaye, if they learned together for long enough, Jerry would understand that love had little to do with acquiring or taking.

"Are you telling me that I don't know what love is?"

"Probably," replied Kaye sadly but with a smile that distanced any form of disapproval or reproach.

"One thing I can tell you for the moment. Contrary to your previous belief that happiness comes from what you can go out and get, one of the best ways to ensure happiness comes from love, but it must be real love. Love is the soil from which happiness grows. The richer the soil, the more robust is the growth. But one of the things that we will learn together, my dear Jerry," said the Mystic with a smile, "is that real love is about giving and not about taking."

The Mystic went on to explain that really the problem was one of terminology. The word "love" was used to describe two distinct states.

The first was the state of taking and consuming.

"When a person says that he loves a kind of food or activity, he is really talking about taking that food or activity for self-gratification. 'I love chocolate' really means I love me and want to gratify myself. There is, of course, nothing wrong with this; the problem is that society describes this activity of self-gratification as 'loving' the object of gratification.

"The second form of love is the way, for example, a parent feels toward his or her child. This form of love is a giving form of love. The greatest product of this love is the opposite of the parent wanting gratification for himself but rather the independence of that child.

"Society confuses these two emotional directions. People assume that the taking and the giving are one thing. In fact, they are entirely separate, and the love which grows happiness is the giving form of love, not the taking form of love. The taking form of love, self-gratification, paradoxically denies a person happiness when carried to extreme. The giving kind of love can have no limit, and happiness is increased proportionately with the giving."

"I just thought of something," said Jerry. "Hollywood endings. For example, there's one very famous movie where the hero meets up with his former girlfriend, who's now married to someone else. All through the movie, the audience is wondering whether she will go back to the first guy, and they're still clearly in love, or will she stay with the man she's married to. At the end of the movie, the hero tells the woman to stay with her husband, and there isn't a dry eye in the theater. Remember, this is a Hollywood movie! I always wondered what I would have done. I can't imagine telling a woman I loved to go away. She's like chocolate; you want to eat it, wrapper and all! Maybe if she had been his child."

"Is Rafaela really only chocolate to you?" said Kaye. "If so, we have a lot of work to do in other directions."

"No, of course not," said Jerry. "I didn't mean it that way."

"What you meant is clear; you are just leaving out that the magic of love of a spouse contains both directions, and they are not a contradiction."

"Right," said Jerry, "I suppose in the movie, it was making a contradiction, with one direction eclipsing the other, that confused me."

Then, characteristically, the Mystic made Jerry feel better by pointing out how much better at giving Jerry had become.

Chapter 14

Jerry's son Sam was at his bedside, pressing him to walk in accordance with the doctor's instructions. With a sigh of consent, Jerry began the process of getting out of bed while Sam unplugged the wires to the drip and took control of steering the column on wheels holding the drip.

They walked for a while in silence. Then Sam, choking back tears, said, "Daddy, you gave us such a fright."

Jerry looked lovingly at his son and said, "Me too, Sam."

"You have always been my rock, and I couldn't manage without you, so you better get well," Sam said with a grim half smile.

Jerry immediately remembered a lesson from the Mystic and now, after all those years, wondered if he should tell his son. It had become important to him, but Sam might just think he was preaching —something Jerry had learned to contain in front of know-it-all children. Of course, the children knew much of what Jerry had learned because inevitably they had been to yeshivas and seminaries as a result of Kaye's prompting. Their starting positions were altogether totally different from that of Jerry and Rafaela and therefore were familiar with many of the things Jerry tried to repeat and which they labeled "Preaching, Dad." Nevertheless, Jerry decided to paraphrase something the Mystic had taught him, first checking whether his son had a mind to listen.

"Sure, Dad, go ahead."

"Well, one day, Kaye was teaching me about how we pray. In the central one of the prayers we say three times a day, we need to be standing."

"Of course," nodded Sam with knowledge which would have been unavailable to Jerry at his age.

"The question the Code of Jewish Law considers is: 'What is standing?'

"What if you are leaning on your table or lectern? Is that standing? Do you have to be in such a position where you are not touching anything to be standing? Is that touching or leaning? What defines 'standing'?

"The answer, of course, is one of degree. If you are leaning gently on your table or lectern, you are still 'standing,' but if you are leaning so heavily that if it were pulled away, you would fall—that is not 'standing.'

"Kaye always emphasized the point that a person has to stand on his own two feet. He cannot lean. Of course, everyone leans to some extent: some on their money or power or prestige, some on their spouse, parents, or even children. Some leaning is natural and to be expected. The test is, what happens to a person if the object leaned on is withdrawn. Does he stay standing, or does he collapse? How many people commit suicide if they lose their money or their spouse or whatever is so precious to them that they have accustomed themselves to lean on it totally?

"But Kaye used to say there was one exception to this. The exception is G-d. In fact, here, we lean as heavily as we can. And you know why, Sam?"

"G-d will never pull away," said Sam with a smile.

"That's right," said Jerry. The things that came so much more easily to his children, who grew up with these concepts, were nonetheless clear to Jerry as a result of his years of slowly absorbing the Mystic's wisdom.

"Let's from now on both stand separately without leaning, son. Neither of us needs to lean on the other."

"Just lean on G-d?"

"Right, Sam, both of us."

Sam kept walking and after a few seconds said, "Whatever, Dad. You are still my rock and I need you, so don't go doing anything stupid."

They continued their walking in silence, the only sound the squeak of the castors rolling the drip.

Chapter 15

Now that Jerry had developed a regimen of walking in the hospital corridors, it was only natural that he would remember the occasions when the Mystic would insist on their walking together. By this time in their relationship, Jerry was ready to tackle some more "advanced" questions.

"We've danced around the topic many times, but I need to ask you some questions on belief in G-d."

"Ask away," Kaye replied, nodding.

"How come there are so many religions in the world, all of whom believe they have a proprietary right to their belief system and that everybody else is wrong? How can there be one G-d if everybody's G-d is totally different? Which G-d do you believe in?"

Jerry always wondered if there would come a time when the Mystic would be stumped, unable to answer, but it never happened.

"So many questions rolled together. Perhaps the easiest is to begin with the fundamental."

Kaye described how everything in the physical world was in a way a mirror image of what existed in the spiritual. Just as there was a sun, for example, the center of our solar system, which nourishes life through the giving of light and warmth, so, too, there is G-d, who enlivens and sustains the world every moment. Just as it is impossible to inspect the sun, it is impossible to inspect G-d. Just as the sun is evident as a result of its shining, so, too, G-d is evident as a result of His shining.

Kaye asked Jerry to imagine a house with many rooms. Each one had different exposures to the light. Some had windows with stained or colored glass; some were in the center of the building with no windows at all. Kaye explained that each of those rooms would have a different level of light, and each of those rooms would have the light colored by the physical structure of that room. Where the window was tinted green, the light would be greener and softer. Where there was a mosaic of color, the light in the room would be dappled over the walls in groups of color. Kaye explained that, nonetheless, there was still only one sun and only one source of light. Mankind had built a world with many rooms and many colored windows. The windows affected how the light came through, but the light was a constant; it was always the same and could be relied upon to be always the same.

The error of many people was that they worshipped the colors of the light on the wall without understanding that they were seeing a man-made refraction of the pure light outside.

Man's job, explained the Mystic, was to go outside his own room and recognize the real light for what it is. Building private sculptures out of colored glass inside the room only distorts the light to fit private tastes of color.

They had reached the top of a hill, and Kaye motioned to sit down on a park bench screened by the cool shade of a huge oak tree. They both sat, Jerry more easily than Kaye, who had his eyes closed, obviously relieved to be resting.

"When it comes to other religions, Jerry," said the Mystic, "there's a lot of confusion out there."

Jerry, used to the pauses that punctuated their time together, waited patiently for Kaye to continue, seemingly to change the subject entirely.

"Is there a difference between power and influence, Jerry?"

Jerry had never thought about it. He tried to see a difference, but what? Powerful men were influential. Influential men were powerful. Bill Gates? The president of the USA? The queen of England? All seemed both. When he gave those examples, Kaye signaled his disagreement.

"The difference is enormous, but once you appreciate what it is, you can understand the four keys we will soon learn," said Kaye.

"Let us suppose you open a business, and it becomes successful and then more and more successful. As it grows, profits rise. Your buying power becomes stronger and stronger. Almost unknown to you at first, you discover this success brings you power. People step out of the way for you, motion for you to go ahead through doors, contradict you less and even not at all; your word is gradually something people listen to, and you are even quoted regularly."

"Bring it on!"

The Mystic ignored the interruption.

"Now suppose you appoint a board to your business. Each director has a vote, and each director is responsible for another part of the business. Can you see you have now *lost* power? In fact, the more the power is divided, the less remains to the person sharing it."

"Yes, I see."

"Now, what about influence? When you influence your child to do good, is your goodness reduced? When you influence your family, your neighborhood, the people you do business with, are you dividing anything? If you light a second candle with yours, are you left with less light? And if that candle lights another and another and another, won't there be more and more light?"

"Got it."

"Power is a problem. The more power a person has, the more difficult it is to share it. The most evil scourges to mankind, Hitler, Stalin, Pol Pot, and so on, murdered without conscience to achieve power and increase their killing to maintain it.

"When a man serves his G-d by fulfilling his mission to be a moral imperative in the world, his influence creates more goodness. Genuine, sincere effort to be good and kind is a process whereby one candle lights another.

"As we learned with hands and feet, just as a hand is not better than a foot and a foot is not better than, but different from, a hand, so it is with Judaism and other religions. Our job is to be a Jew and not be concerned with other disciplines. We have our unique role, and a non-Jew has his own sacred and vital role. In fulfilling our role, the pursuit is influence, not power."

Jerry nodded understanding. Both men sat caressed by the breeze, neither ready to get up.

After some minutes of silence, the Mystic said:

"There is a story about a poor Jew named R. Isaac, who lived in a small village with his wife and children. He began having dreams about finding a treasure buried under a bridge in a faraway city. He decided to try his luck, and, undeterred by his wife's protests, set out to find the treasure. He found the city, he found the bridge, but it was heavily guarded by the local police. He began to dig, but the police immediately stopped him. Rather than go to prison, he was forced to explain what he was doing. One of the policemen laughed at him. He too had a dream, that a pile of gold was buried in the backyard of a simple Jew named R. Isaac, who lived in a small village faraway. But he, the policeman, was not foolish enough to waste his time going on a wild goose chase.

"As soon as R. Isaac was released, he hurried home. He dug and he dug in his yard, and, sure enough, there, hidden under the chicken coop, was an enormous sack of gold that some robber had buried there a long time ago for safekeeping."

"Nice story," said Jerry.

"The point is, of course," continued the Mystic, "your inquiry about other religions is answered for a Jew by R. Isaac's experience—that real spiritual fortune is found at home, not in some faraway place, as so many assume, and that furthermore, that spiritual fortune needs to be passed on by influence, not divided as power."

How Jerry had grown to love the Mystic!

Chapter 16

Jerry remembered vividly the time when the Mystic told him that he might be leaving the city in which Jerry lived.

Jerry had felt fear clutch at his heart at the thought of being deprived of the security of the sessions with the Mystic. Apparently, the Mystic's teaching job was in jeopardy.

Kaye was a teacher of small children in a charitable institution. The head of the charitable institution was rumored to have committed some kind of fraud, the details of which were still unclear. If that fraud came to light, apparently the institution would be closed down, and therefore, there would be no salary for the Mystic.

Jerry remonstrated with Kaye that he could get another job, presumably a better-paying job. Kaye explained that he wasn't interested in the better pay; he was interested in having light and clean work that would allow him time to further his mystical studies and fulfill his obligations to impart his wisdom to others.

Kaye reminded Jerry that he had often been puzzled at Kaye's severity with himself in relation to physical pleasures such as eating and drinking. The Mystic took it upon himself to explain that there are various levels in a person's growth to spiritual maturity. No man, explained Kaye, was the age on his passport in spiritual terms. Spiritual advancement required effort and exercise in exactly the same way that physical effort and exercise strengthened the muscles in our bodies. In order to produce robust spiritual muscle, time and effort must be spent pursuing spiritual pursuits. Those things on their own were helpful but insufficient. Since, as the Mystic often explained, action is the main thing, there needed to be added into the spiritual exercise regime a program of doing positive good for other people on a regular and meaningful basis.

Kaye explained to Jerry that one of the difficulties in making spiritual advancement was that the spiritual and the physical had difficulty coexisting. He explained by giving as an example a glass of wine. If, in front of you, there is an empty glass, the glass can be filled with wine. If, however, the glass is filled with water, there is no place in which to put the wine. The Mystic explained to Jerry that a man is like a glass; he can either be filled with physical preoccupations: food, drink, money, power, achievement, etc.—in which case his glass is full of one kind of existence—or he can seek wisdom through contemplation and prayer and work for the benefit of mankind, which would also elevate his own soul in the process. One was water, one was wine, but a full glass of water and a full glass of wine cannot both coexist in the same empty glass. The less water, the more room for wine, and vice versa.

The Mystic reminded Jerry that he had once told him to keep enjoying his ice cream. In other words, he should keep continuing to focus on those physical things that he needed for his life: food, drink, money, power, achievement, and the like because he was not ready yet to do without any of these things or to even begin minimizing them. The Mystic gently told Jerry, however, that there would come a time when he would himself feel ready to surrender some of that list in exchange for some of the contemplation, prayer, and action for others that would replace it.

Jerry learned this lesson well over the years and committed to the journey with resulting steady progress. Meanwhile, he could still not come to terms with the thought of the Mystic leaving him. His fear at not having the guidance he had become used to was so complete that he felt his heart thumping in his chest as he heard himself asking the Mystic how it was possible that the head of the charitable organization, who himself was a deeply learned scholar, could get to the point where he was doing something so dishonest.

The Mystic smiled at him kindly and told him to be gentle when judging. He explained to Jerry that you could never judge until you were in someone else's position, and, since every soul was in every body for its own unique growth program, no two people were really ever in the same position, which made a judgment next to impossible. The Mystic went on to explain a parable.

"Suppose that one day, a man who was covered in muck came to your house, tried to break into your home, and wanted to kidnap your children. You would have no choice but to stop him any way you could. In doing so, you would definitely get filthy yourself, but you would have no choice in the matter.

"The man in charge of our institution is a good and clever man. Life is a difficult experience with thousands of daily challenges and problems. There are times when men fail. There are times when, having to deal with the problems of life in winning a particular fight, we find ourselves covered in dirt. No matter how much we try, we may never get it all off."

"How have you always managed?" asked Jerry.

"I have not been tested," said the Mystic with simple truth.

"I spend my time in solitude and in teaching.

I'm therefore not tested by having to deal with the villains of the world and am free to pursue spiritual growth and try to assist others in doing so. I have no idea whether if I were tested the way the head of our institution has been, I would do better or worse."

Jerry remembered that they were walking down his favorite tree-lined street. They walked in silence until the Mystic continued, returning to the subject of integrity.

"I was very proud of you when I learned you didn't inflate the insurance claim."

"How did you find out?" asked Jerry.

"Rafaela told me with the same pride," said Kaye.

Kaye then went on to explain to Jerry that he was, although proud, not sure that Jerry really understood the issue of integrity and self-esteem.

He began to explain to Jerry that most of society was confused in relation to self-esteem, which they recognized as a positive, on one hand, and arrogance and boasting on the other, which they thought of, quite rightly, as a negative. Furthermore, commercial life required the business of blowing one's own trumpet and the business of communicating to others an inflated perspective. After a series of questions, Kaye told Jerry that he thought it was important that they learn the differences together.

Kaye began explaining to Jerry that self-esteem was a great positive and fundamental in the preparation for personal happiness. Everyone was obligated to find out his own talents and his own abilities. There is no profit in pretending that we do not have abilities that have been granted to us.

Conversely, we need to know our limitations and understand that those limitations may be imposed by our genetic inheritance or environment. It was stupid to be ashamed of any such limitation.

As he had explained with the story of R. Zusha, the important thing was to use our talents responsibly. At no point, however, does this prevent a man from knowing his strengths and weaknesses. Men who are best suited for a job have to know that they are indeed best suited. It then only becomes an issue of whether the responsibility is being discharged to full advantage. There is no sense whatsoever in pretending that G-d-given talents don't exist or, conversely, that we do not have our limitations. The Mystic used the example of a man being tall or short. If he is short, he should recognize that fact and not say that he is tall. That is self-esteem, which is consistent with truth.

If, however, a man who is short pretends to be tall or tells others that he is tall or pretends to himself that he is tall, this is a lie and is arrogance and boasting. Even if a man knows he is tall, which is the truth, but confuses this with his achievement, this is also arrogance. The pride that he has in being tall is not based on anything that he has achieved; it is simply pride in a G-d-given reality. There is, therefore, nothing to be proud of and nothing to boast about. The issue is: does the man use his height for the purpose of exploiting his other talents to the best of his ability or not?

It is one of the great secrets of internal peace that a man or woman learns to have genuine self-esteem and discards the ugly and negative aspects of boasting and arrogance. One of the steps in establishing a real sense of self-esteem is the difficulty in finding and keeping personal truth, and that is a matter of developing a sense of personal integrity. Separating talents and achievements allow for real self-esteem, which in turn contributes to a man's internal sense of rest.

Why it was so important not to cheat the insurance company, explained the Mystic, was that the additional money yielded by the cheating, even assuming that it was ultimately successful, was simply too expensive. The cost of the profit was the cost of your personal view of your own integrity. A personal view of tarnished integrity results in the automatic loss of self-esteem.

Chapter 17

One thing always amazed Jerry about his rabbi friend. No matter what event in his life Jerry wanted to discuss, the Mystic would find a way to connect it to some important life lesson. Once, as they walked, Kaye noticed Jerry was more quiet than usual with his questions.

"Is anything wrong?" asked Kaye gently.

"Not really," replied Jerry inaccurately. "It is just that I have an old friend who, I learned today, is being divorced by his wife."

The Mystic nodded in support, and Jerry continued to describe the friend and his wife. Both were psychiatrists, both intelligent and of good character. They simply, as the story was told to Jerry, could not live together.

Kaye was silent for a while and then asked, "Have I ever talked to you about the notion of *tzimtzum* (contraction)?"

"No."

"Although the notion comes from profound Kabbalah, it is now a fundamental concept in Chasidut, which is what we learn together. This is as good a time as any to understand this idea. It is a difficult concept, consistent in a way with the Big Bang Theory. Kabbalists explain that 'before' Creation, there was only the blaze of G-dliness. Nothing else existed, and it was logically impossible for anything else to exist because nothing could withstand the intensity inherent in the unity of G-dliness. When G-d decided to create the world, it was necessary first to 'contract' Himself, as it were, in order to make 'room' for physical existence. Into this 'contracted' spiritual 'space,' it became possible for something apparently separate from G-dliness to exist. There are complex Kabbalistic steps from there to the world as we know it, but something that is almost unfathomable comes from this information."

The Mystic paused, waiting to see if Jerry was following. Satisfied, he continued.

"When there is a fundamental truth in the Torah, that fundamental truth exists across all of creation."

"Such as?" asked Jerry.

"OK. Take the example, 'It was evening, it was morning, one day.' Are you familiar with that statement in the account of Creation?"

"Sure."

"This becomes a rule in life. Dark precedes light. Descent precedes ascent, as we will see when you learn the four keys. Order comes from chaos. The given is the chaos; the mission is to make from it order."

"OK."

"Just as it is a truth that for creation to exist, G-d must first 'contract' Himself, this becomes so for every case of giver and receiver. So, in order for our world to have a separate existence and receive its nourishment from the Almighty, first there must be a contraction in the Almighty's light, and this process must occur whenever light needs to be passed on."

"For example?" asked Jerry.

"For example, you and me," explained the Mystic.

"In order for me to communicate something from my learning to you, I must first contract it to a bite size you can digest. The more I contract it, the more likely you are to be able to understand it. Conversely, suppose I wanted to know something about the intricacies of title transfer. If you described your total knowledge to me in one go, I would have no chance of taking it in. It is a paradox that the more the light is diffused by the giver, the more it has the chance of being transferred to the receiver. The more contraction in the giver, the more expansion in the receiver."

"Incredible but true," observed Jerry. "It's the same with my children. If I want to explain something to them, I have to bring it down to their level so they would understand."

"Yes," said Kaye.

"Of course, your children can then work with the new information and expand it."

"Right," said Jerry.

The two men walked in silence for some time. Jerry sensed there was more to come, wondering what this had to do with his friend and the divorce.

"Do you see that a truth is a constant, Jerry? This truth holds true in relationships as well. Take a husband and wife. If the wife is to flourish, the husband needs to be contracted to whatever extent is needed for her to have room to function and vice versa. The same is true in all relationships. A boss will only get the best out of an employee by according him or her space for initiative."

So this was the marriage lesson. If only the whole world could learn to live from the Mystic! Jerry understood the lesson and was determined not to go the way of his friend who, he suddenly realized, had been totally suffocating his poor wife.

Chapter 18

The more Jerry walked around the hospital halls by day and spent hours lying in his bed awake at night, the more he was flooded with memories of the Mystic. It was when Jerry was nearing fifty years of age that he began to lose money. There was a fall in the property market, which destroyed his whole financial structure. Although his law firm specialized in top-of-the-market commercial realty and he had become an expert in the field, the market crash laughed at his careful, sophisticated planning.

Until Jerry recouped his losses years later, without the Mystic, he could never have survived the roller coaster ride from wealth to the trap door of bankruptcy. It was amazing, mused Jerry in the hospital, that with Kaye's constant help throughout the painful contraction process, he had succeeded in avoiding serious worry. It had taken fifteen years of training with the Mystic to reach the point where he had learned how to do this. There were times on the way down, however, when Jerry faltered. One such time, he had been called in to the bank from which he and some partners had taken substantial loans to hear his financial death sentence. He sat in the waiting room of the office of the so-called "Special Borrowers' Section," trembling. After waiting half an hour under increasing tension and pressure, Jerry was told by the bank manager's PA that regrettably, he would have to cancel the appointment, and the time was rescheduled for the next week. Relieved and jubilant that the meeting had been postponed, Jerry went home to some good Scotch whiskey.

That evening, Kaye made an unexpected visit. It was as if he knew to come, that Jerry desperately needed him. His stated reason was that he had come to leave a book with Jerry, but he was quick to observe that Jerry looked unusually unsettled and asked after Jerry's welfare. Jerry explained that he had been scheduled for a heavy meeting with his bankers, at which time he would have had to "face the music" for a series of substantially overdue loan payments. His entire financial well-being would have been over, and, as he had had a reprieve, he was celebrating with his friend Johnny Walker.

The Mystic was quiet for a few moments and then asked if he could stay a little while. Jerry, delighted to have the comfort, immediately agreed. Predictably, Kaye refused to join Jerry in the Scotch.

After commiserating with Jerry about the stress, Kaye prompted him to remember the real perspective and asked why he had not used the four keys.

The four keys were the method of thought and perspective that the Mystic had taught Jerry and which, when used properly, freed a person from the worries of everyday living. Jerry looked at Kaye and sheepishly explained that since his entire financial ruin rested upon that meeting, he could not help being totally intimidated, so he lost sight of any sublime perspectives.

Kaye was silent and then asked Jerry, "Do you know what a pierced-ear slave is?"

"No," replied Jerry.

"A pierced-ear slave is the description given to a slave, really an indentured servant, who refuses to access his freedom. The Torah presents a series of complex laws in relation to how and when the man was to go free, whether with or without a wife, whether with or without children, whether with or without property, and so forth. Sometimes, however, his life as a slave was so good, or so safe, that he did not want his freedom. Instead, therefore, he had the right to elect to remain a slave with the master from that point onward for the rest of his life. If he chose to remain a slave, he was marked by having his earlobe pierced so that everybody could have notice of his status."

The Mystic paused.

"Freedom is so precious at a physical level that people will fight for it, sacrifice for it, and even die for it, yet at a spiritual level, people just despair of it because it is even harder to obtain. It requires great effort and constant perspective adjustment.

"So the question that I'm asking you now that

you have the four keys and are refusing to access the wisdoms locked behind each of them is, do you really want to be a pierced-ear slave?"

Jerry did not need any more Scotch that night. The Mystic had guided him firmly back on track with the lessons he had learned.

He remembered how long it had taken him to learn the four keys and how much discussion was required. If only he had the Mystic to help him use the keys now that he had to address dying.

Chapter 19

Two routines to which Jerry became quickly accustomed in the hospital were the changing of the swabs in the wound on his stomach and the daily shower.

As far as the wound was concerned, Jerry had a long incision which ended at the navel. The incision was packed with gauze soaked in disinfectant, over which was taped a kind of fabric patch. Three times a day, a tag team of nursing staff came and unceremoniously tore off the patch and then redressed the wound.

The number of nurses was bewildering and varied dramatically in terms of age, nationality, and skin color., Each nurse seemed to do things his or her own way, each one lamenting the job that had been done by the person before.

What was consistent with every visit was the pain. Irrespective of the individual differences of the nursing contingent, the agony was always the same and required fifteen or twenty minutes' respite for it to go away.

The other routine, although not painful, was equally unpleasant. Every morning, Jerry was separated from the drip to be coaxed into the shower by one of the male nurses. The inequality of the nurse being fully dressed and Jerry being naked remained incongruous every day. The various shower nurses, some huge, some diminutive, all showered Jerry in a consistent manner. Water was run from the handheld shower hose and tested as being lukewarm on the nurse's arm. Jerry was then commanded to find his way, with the nurse's help, to the plastic chair in the shower recess. There, the nurse unceremoniously soaked and rinsed Jerry as though washing his car. Any attempt at conversation or humor was met with stony silence and an expression of dedication to the task of getting the "car" as clean as possible with a minimum amount of time and effort. Each shower left Jerry needing recovery time as well. It was during these rests that Jerry's mind drifted to the four keys.

One of the outstanding memories of Jerry's life was the day, in the garden under the avocado tree, that the Mystic finally accepted that Jerry was ready to understand the importance of the four keys, the first of which he had alluded to on several occasions. The Mystic now explained to him that the first of these keys was fundamental to any level of spiritual advancement. It was also the first of the tools that allowed Joseph to be happy even in prison in a way that was *not* responsive. It was also the first huge clue in building a personal mission statement.

To prove his point, Kaye provided the following demonstration. He asked Jerry to picture a painting, and Jerry chose the Mona Lisa.

"Describe it to me with your eyes closed," said the Mystic.

Jerry closed his eyes and began trying to recall what the painting actually looked like. He described the shape of her face, the famous smile, her arms folded in her lap, the winding road in the background, the color of her hair.... Suddenly, there was a loud crash, and Jerry sat up startled, his eyes wide open. Kaye had slammed his open palm on the tea table with as much force as he could muster, startling Jerry with the shock.

"What happened to the picture?"

"Gone," admitted Jerry.

The Mystic began to explain that, just as Jerry had created a miniature world in his mind, G-d, as it were, pictures everything in Creation and thus causes it to be. Just as Jerry had been 'creating' the picture in his mind by 'focusing' on it, so does G-d actually create everything in physical existence by 'focusing' on it. If G-d were to interrupt that focus for even a microsecond, existence would end. Of course, for G-d, this is effortless; there is no interruption in the creative process. What Jerry needed to understand, explained the Mystic, was that creation was a continuous and ongoing process from microsecond to microsecond.

Jerry remained unexcited by this news and, even allowing it to be true, could not yet see why it was so important.

The Mystic went on to explain.

"The mere fact that focus is required entails *control*. Just as you were controlling the picture in your mind's eye when you were picturing the winding road, G-d, as it were, controls everything that He is bringing into creation. You will understand this by understanding that if He wasn't, it wouldn't exist. That means that every tree needs to be thought of at every moment; otherwise, those trees would not exist. That is true for people, animals, plants, inert matter; in short, the whole of creation. If each and every blade of grass was not focused on, it would not exist. If each and every hair on your head or your arm was not focused on, it would not exist. The whole of creation is absolutely Divinely controlled. This in turn means that everything that happens is "purposeful," meaning that there can be no such thing as random happenstance. There can be no such thing as coincidence. You and I may not understand *why* something is happening, but we *must* understand that it is happening *purposefully*. The variables in creation are so many and so vast, as we will learn separately, that we have no way of possibly tracking and collating why things are happening when they are. The important thing in this stage of your development is for you to understand that nothing happens by chance; in fact, there can be no such thing as chance."

"Isn't that fatalism?" Jerry remembered asking, clearly not satisfied.

"No," replied the Mystic.

"Man is a partner in creation and has free choice. His free choice is one of the factors influencing how the creative process is regenerated. There is no question that he is an influencer, but there is equally no question that the background and environment and circumstances that happen to man are absolutely and totally Divinely controlled.

"If this is really understood," whispered Kaye, "there can be no fear."

Jerry felt a shiver down his back as Kaye leaned forward, looking at him intently.

"Do you understand that if G-d is bringing every circumstance into creation purposefully, and if G-d is all good, there can be no room for fear? There can be no room for worry. There can be no room for anxiety. This is the springboard to learning trust. These are all separate and difficult concepts, but for the moment, do you understand that if G-d is recreating every single microbe, atom, and molecule in creation purposefully and guiding its movement and influence, and if, furthermore, G-d is doing all of this for good, even though we do not understand that good at the moment, there can be no room for any fear or worry?"

"Yes," said Jerry, "I see that."

"Are you telling me you are never afraid?" asked Jerry.

"Yes," said the Mystic.

"Are you telling me you are never anxious?" asked Jerry.

"Yes," said the Mystic.

"Are you telling me that you never worry?" asked Jerry.

"Yes, I'm telling you all of those things," said the Mystic, "but I'm telling you something much more important than that. I'm telling you that it is available to *you* not to be frightened or anxious or worried about anything ever again. It is simply a matter of your effort in learning to focus on what you've learned today."

"So, do we have free choice or not?"

"We do, but this is much misunderstood. We have no free choice as to what happens *to* us. We have absolute free choice in relation to how we *react* to it.

"What happens *to* us is a matter of Divine Providence, as we have just learned. It is true that this Divine Providence is influenced by our behavior, but the fact remains that what happens *to* us is deliberate, controlled, and for the good. How *we react* is a matter of free choice.

"This key is fundamental to the next three keys. It is the mental fallback position and the basis of all trust and faith.

"This is the formula for the first key. But Jerry,"

"Yes?"

"You will have to make the key yourself, and you will then need to use it yourself."

Jerry now, after so many years of use, closely cherished and guarded this first well-made and well-worn key.

Chapter 20

"The second of the keys follows from the first," explained the Mystic.

"Let me pose a huge question to you, Jerry. If everything in creation is purposeful and there are no accidents or coincidences, and everything G-d does is for the good, why is it that apparently negative things continue to challenge mankind in general and you, Jerry, in particular?"

Kaye had long walked with difficulty and puffed as he spoke, steadied from time to time by Jerry's arm.

The Mystic then began to explain the second key. He squeezed Jerry's arm for emphasis as he explained that all descent is for the purpose of ascent. He paused meaningfully as his words sank in.

Most people, without the keys that the Mystic was giving to Jerry, viewed descent as bad luck or bad management resulting in a negative, which was the conclusion of whatever had happened. Instead, explained Kaye, the negative needs to be seen as only part of the process, and the process needs to continue through the negative into a subsequent positive. Since every descent was for the purpose of an ascent, it followed from that descent was the potential for a subsequent ascent. Indeed, the Mystic explained, there were really no major ascents in life without the preparatory beginning of a descent first.

"Wow," said Jerry.

"Think back over your life, Jerry. Every real growth must have come from a prior perceived setback. I say 'perceived' because there is no such thing. Every descent is given to us as an opportunity for ascent."

The Mystic explained there were a few difficult stages in the acquisition of this second key.

The first—and this required much training—

was to understand that any perceived bad is a mirage. The very thing that disappoints is the potential for good. It may be that one doesn't see it yet, but it is so anyway and invariably. Whenever something negative happens, apart from its discomfort or pain, there will be now or in the future an opportunity for ascent. With training, when this ascent actually takes place, it is important to be able to look back and understand that the prior descent was the first step in the ultimate triumph of the ascent.

The second and much more difficult stage, explained Kaye (and this took years of preparatory thought and discipline), was to understand that, even when descending, the very descent was actually part of some subsequent unknown ascent.

People not privy to this secret, the Mystic explained, continued to curse their bad fortune or management whenever a reversal of their fortune took place. People, on the other hand, aware of this secret, understood that the very reversal was a potential for new growth and new achievement.

Kaye assured Jerry that if he examined people who had reached milestones in their life, they would, if sensitive to observing the past truthfully, have had a signpost of descent before they reached the height of their ascent. This is true in business, where people may fail in one area only to change to another and do disproportionately better, or where people missed out on opportunities thought to be marvelous only to find that the opportunity, had it been pursued, would have been harmful, destructive, or at best disappointing. Examples of this were legion and endless.

Jerry remembered the beautiful story the Mystic told him to illustrate his point. He told him that there was a man known as R. Gavriel, who was one of the most prominent Jews in Vitebsk. Twenty-five years after their marriage, he and his wife were still childless. Then, by reason of sustained persecution, he became impoverished. He was understandably upset, therefore, when an appeal reached him from R. Schneur Zalman of Liadi to participate in a case of redeeming Jewish captives with a substantial contribution, as he was wont to do in former days, but which was now far beyond his means. When his wife learned of her husband's predicament, she sold her jewelry and raised the required amount. Then she scrubbed and polished the coins until they gleamed brightly, and with a prayer in her heart that their *mazal* might brighten up, she wrapped the coins in a bundle, which she handed over to her husband to take to R. Schneur Zalman.

Coming into the presence of R. Schneur Zalman, R. Gavriel placed the bundle of money on the table. R. Schneur Zalman told him to open it. At once, the coins shone with an extraordinary brilliance.

R. Schneur Zalman became engrossed in thought, then said: "Of all the gold, silver, and brass which the Jews contributed to the Mishkan (Sanctuary), nothing shone so brightly as the washbasin and its stand (which were made of the brass mirrors contributed by the Jewish women with selflessness and joy).

"Tell me, where did you get these coins?"

R. Gavriel revealed to R. Schneur Zalman the state of his affairs and how his wife, Chana Rivka bas Beila, had raised the money.

R. Schneur Zalman placed his head on his hands and for some time was in deep contemplation. Then he lifted his head and bestowed on R. Gavriel and his wife the blessing of children, long life, riches, and extraordinary grace. He told R. Gavriel to close his business in Vitebsk and to begin to trade in precious gems and diamonds.

R. Schneur Zalman's blessing was fulfilled. R. Gavriel Nosei-Chein became wealthy. He and his wife were also blessed with sons and daughters.

He lived to the age of 110 years, and his wife survived him by two years.

Jerry remembered that Kaye had stopped for breath. When Jerry was about to speak, the Mystic silenced him by continuing.

"Now, Jerry, consider this. Which of the things that happened to Gavriel would have appeared to him at the time as 'good'?"

"Obviously the success of the new business and the birth of a child," said Jerry.

"Sure. What of meeting R. Schneur Zalman, who gave him the advice to change his business?"

"Good," agreed Jerry.

"What about using his last coin to ransom a captive, leaving him destitute?"

Jerry hesitated. "Maybe not good at the time."

"Exactly," replied Kaye, beaming, "and later?"

"Good."

"What about his failing business?"

"I understand," said Jerry.

"You are saying without the bad of losing money, there would be no later good, so the losing of the money was in fact good, not bad."

"You have it," said Kaye, drawing breath in a way Jerry had learned was a preface to something important.

"That is only a first step. It is, admittedly, an imperative step, but a first step nonetheless. This step becomes the key with the realization and trust that what seems 'bad' is actually *necessarily* the gateway to subsequent growth and flowering of revealed good. Put another way, every descent is for the purpose of ascent.

"The first two keys on their own are very powerful, Jerry," said the Mystic carefully and quietly. "If you know that everything is being Divinely controlled around you, and if you know that when you are experiencing a negative, it is going to be an opportunity for your growth and your development, you will be armed with a robust and optimistic outlook in relation to anything you do. Furthermore, whenever you experience disappointment or pain or even, G-d forbid, suffering, you will know that this is happening to you by design and you will know that it is for your benefit and growth.

"Most difficult for many people, even if they have these keys, is to accept the responsibility of moving forward and actually growing in practice. Remember, Jerry, as I always tell you, action is the main thing."

In the next few sessions, Jerry remembered. The Mystic refused new information, patiently instead questioning Jerry on the extent to which he understood the first two keys of absolute Divine Providence and every descent being for the sake of ascent.

Chapter 21

One more day left, thought Jerry on the morning of the fourth day. He had been swabbed, had his dressing changed, and showered. Jerry lay propped up on crisp, newly changed pillows in his crisp, newly changed bed. Tomorrow, thought Jerry, I will know whether I'm going to die. What sort of ascent is possible after the descent of death? These were all issues of the afterlife which, being non-provable, were little comfort to many people.

When Jerry lost his money ten-odd years ago, the precious keys kept him from fear, worry, and even distress. Now that he was in the hospital, he was able to use these tools to understand that the cancer and the operation must have been Divinely orchestrated and must be a descent for the purpose of an ascent. But what was the ascent? None as far as Jerry was concerned. Jerry forced himself to consider the third key.

There was an interval of about a year between the time that the Mystic taught Jerry the second key and the time that he spoke to Jerry for the first time about the third. The reason for this, according to Kaye, was that he was insistent on observing how Jerry was assimilating the information and then how he was putting it to use.

By the time Jerry had lost his money and before he had remade much of it, he was in possession of all four keys, which allowed him to move through the process of loss the way even Kaye may have done himself.

The institution for which Kaye worked in fact survived the threat of scandal, which panicked Jerry some years before. It was found that the head of the institution was innocent of the allegations against him. As a result, Kaye was able to stay on at his post and, to Jerry's great relief, continue to be his teacher.

The mere fact of the possibility that he might leave made Jerry consider carefully his teacher's financial position for the first time. Kaye was obviously living at a very simple level and, with his many children and grandchildren, this must have been difficult. Any effort to support Kaye financially, however, was met with constant and unarguable refusal. It had been Rafaela who had the kind and clever idea of giving money to Kaye's wife on the condition that Kaye was not to know. Years before Jerry underwent the descent of losing his money in his early fifties, he had made regular transfers of money to the Mystic's wife, and for years, the Mystic had no idea that the money was paid or where it came from. When Kaye found out, he was disappointed that Jerry had not told him, but he understood. This led him to ask:

"Do you remember, Jerry, when we talked about the three blessings?"

"Of course," replied Jerry.

"Do you remember that we talked about whether or not you had the wish to be happy irrespective of the blessings that you had?"

"Yes, I remember," replied Jerry.

"I see that you now appreciate how this is possible," said the Mystic with satisfaction. During the intervening year, the Mystic reminded Jerry of what they had learned as the first two keys: if everything is Divinely controlled and if every descent is for the purpose of ascent, then irrespective of what happens to you at any particular time, there is the potential for growth particular to that situation at that time. This was a very difficult key, warned Kaye, but required this view: *there is that which happens to a person from the outside and there is the manner in which the person is free to react to it from the inside.* If what happens from the outside is perceived as being a random series of painful punches with no further purpose, then it is easy to fall into despair. The events that happen will be divided into those things perceived at the moment as being "good" and those things perceived at the moment as being "bad." The things perceived at the moment as being "good" will cause a level of joy. If, however, a person could train himself to understand that whatever "bad" is happening at a particular moment has the potential for a subsequent good, then that negative can be embraced in the same way as that which appears to be good.

Jerry was asked to repeat and give his own examples. More effectively, the Mystic insisted that Jerry's examples came from current daily life.

Kaye would often repeat:

"Do you remember the story of the Chasid in Siberia?"

"Yes," Jerry would answer.

"Do you see now how he saw his imprisonment? Since it was Divinely orchestrated and *therefore* for his good, he *perceived* the imprisonment as good. The only question was what he should be doing with that good. His conclusion was just as he served G-d at home, so should he serve G-d in Siberia."

"Marvelous," affirmed Jerry.

Kaye would also often repeat:

"Do you remember the story of R. Gavriel?"

"Of course," Jerry would reply.

"Do you remember I quizzed you as to what point do you say that the family's fortune became good? When the wife became pregnant? When they remade their money in gems? When they donated the money to save a life? When their business was in the throes of ruin prior to the giving of the money?"

The Mystic insisted that Jerry review that there are a series of events in everybody's life which are viewed as "good" or "bad" as they happen. We are not equipped, with ordinary sight, to view a series of events in a total context. At the time the business was dissolving, it would have been temping for R. Gavriel and his wife to view this as "bad," which would have made the determination to donate the money so great an effort. It was only the endowment of the coins, which allowed R. Gavriel to meet the person of influence who steered him into the gem business that ultimately became so successful. Yet once this *end* is viewed as "good," all the "bad" things that happened are suddenly revealed as having been good.

Jerry remembered, lying in the hospital bed, that during that year, he had spent a good deal of private time, at golf and alone in the car, thinking of what he had termed to himself as "Kaye time." Although he had to a large extent assimilated the first two keys, he was still unsure of two issues and chose his moment to ask.

"If we are to be so happy with everything that happens to us, why do we pray for pain to stop? Why do we ask for money, health, and children? Anyway, haven't you said over and over again that we are to pray for our needs?"

The Mystic was obviously pleased with the question, showing as it did that Jerry was learning and, more importantly, seeking to apply what he had learned.

"There are two levels of good: one revealed and one concealed. Sometimes, the kindness G-d metes out needs to be hidden as apparent harshness."

"Why?"

"Let's take an example of your daughter sitting on the floor with a fork trying to prod it into the electricity socket. You tell your daughter no, but she continues to try and poke. You take away the fork, but next time she is eating and out of her chair, she tries it again. What do you do? Smiling and kissing won't work. You have to show anger, strictness, severity, so she is scared or inhibited from doing it again. But is there any doubt you love her? In fact, you love her so much, you endure the pain of her pain. This is good concealed as bad.

"Now look at this from the child's perspective. Because the good is not revealed, she wants it to stop. She wants her Daddy kissing her again.

"The example is oversimplified, but we pray for the good to be revealed and the lesson to be over. We, in effect, say to G-d, 'I understand I needed this or that until now, but whatever the benefit, I have it now, so please, from now on, I want the revealed good.'"

Jerry determined to spend Kaye time on this but meanwhile asked his second question.

"Once we are talking of praying for our needs, what is the difference between me asking for your blessing and me praying to G-d—no comparison intended, of course."

"Of course," laughed Kaye. "The difference is infinite.

"On Rosh Hashanah, the year is mapped out for each person in potential. Whether he lives or dies, becomes sick or well, rich or poor."

"So why do we pray every day—if everything

has been determined?" Jerry asked, not disguising his confusion.

"Because," replied the Mystic slowly, "it is there for us in potential only. One still has to bring these blessings down into actuality. Accessing these blessings depends on behavior."

"Ah. How interesting. Now that you put it like that, I see it," said Jerry.

"A mystic can help you actualize your already formed-up potential by advising where you have gone wrong or by giving a blessing, opening the door to the flow of the potential. But when a man prays to G-d, G-d is unlimited. He is not constrained by your potential determined on Rosh Hashanah. He can do, or give, anything He wants."

"Got it," said Jerry.

The Mystic smiled, obviously pleased.

Jerry remembered the next sentence as clearly as hearing the Mystic ask if he was happy all those years ago.

"Next week, we begin the third key."

Chapter 22

"The third key, Jerry, is perspective.

"It is possible," explained Kaye, "to have a perspective that overrides the various incidents that are happening to you from time to time. This is implicit in the first two keys. All is controlled, all is for the best, and every descent is for an ascent. But *seeing* this and having it as a default mindset is a matter of perspective, something that needs to be cultivated and practiced.

"Let's take an example. Suppose a man is forced to carry a load of stones on his back up a mountain on foot. He staggers in the hot sun, sweating under the load. He is resentful and rebellious and suffers. The heavier the load, the more the suffering.

"Now tell this same man he is carrying diamonds in his sack and at the top of the mountain they will be his. Now does he suffer? Now is he elated, rejoicing in every pound he is carrying.

"What has changed? The load is the same, the temperature is the same, the mountain is the same, his strength is the same.

"What has changed is his *perspective*. All the other factors are exactly the same. The difference is that our man *perceives* the weight as good, whereas before, he *perceived* the load as bad.

"Do you see this, Jerry?"

"I do."

"A man has the capacity with this third key of being truly happy all the time. His perspective is that his load is diamonds, even if it seems to be stones. The fact that he can't stop and inspect the diamonds at this particular moment is irrelevant. Sooner or later, when he is able to stop and unpack the bag, the bag will show the content of the stones as being really diamonds. Why? Because the first key proves it is happening deliberately (being forced to carry the stones up the mountain) and for the good, and the second key tells you that any apparent descent (the weight of stones) is really for the purpose of ascent (finding them to be diamonds).

"There is an aspect to this key which is very important," said the Mystic as he looked over Jerry's head toward the horizon. *Know today that no man is tested beyond his capacity to carry the load. The mere fact that some people seem to have terrible tribulations in this world is only because they have souls strong enough and vigorous enough to be able to carry the load.* This third key allows them to acquire the perspective that the load is diamonds, not stones.

"Of course, when a man is being tested, others can take no comfort from this truth. Where another person is concerned, his suffering requires your immediate unconditional help, but for ourselves, the third key of perspective is everything."

Years before, Jerry had internalized a teaching from Kaye on another aspect of perspective. He had learned that in regard to physical benefits, always look at someone with less than you; with spiritual virtues, always look to someone higher than you. He had noticed that most unhappy people have the order reversed. They envy the man with more material wealth and excuse their poor behavior by comparing themselves to someone who has behaved, or does behave, worse. This observation had been a great help to him. But this third key of perspective was something much bigger and much more empowering.

Jerry gave it much Kaye time.

Chapter 23

The fourth key was really easy to learn. Jerry was almost there himself and just needed a clear articulation to understand. The Mystic had become bent from his age, the last year having taken its toll on his health. He walked much more slowly when they walked together and would often take Jerry's arm rather than use a stick. Far from minding, Jerry felt honored to be able to support a soul that he had learned to love deeply. Jerry loved the Mystic's goodness, his kindness, and his firm resolve not to compromise anything he held to be valuable for any short-term gain.

"Like animals, humans are motivated by the pain and pleasure principle, Jerry," Kaye said.

"So the question becomes: what place is there in life for pleasure? Is it to be rejected as the water that fills the glass, preventing the entry of the wine? Is it to be embraced totally as instructed by the idiotic and treacherous saying, 'If it feels good, do it'? Where do we place pleasure in terms of our daily life?

"The key to this was important to apply to the other three keys," continued the Mystic.

"Pleasure and pain both have their uses. Pain is to signal a problem, pleasure to signal a success. It is a success for the body to eat from time to time. It is a success for the body to drink from time to time. It is necessary for the procreation of the human race to enjoy intercourse.

"The issue is," stressed the Mystic, "one of *focus.*" Jerry felt his arm being squeezed gently as Kaye used the word "focus." He felt a flood of satisfaction at the fact that the time that they had spent together was obviously of value to the Mystic. Kaye went on to say that if the focus is on the activity and the pleasure is secondary, then the pleasure is good and healthy and deserved. If the focus is on the pleasure for the pleasure's sake, then the pleasure is perverse. At one end of the spectrum are the ordinary daily pleasures of life, and at the other end of the spectrum, exaggerated pleasures are sought for their own sake.

"I once told you many years ago to enjoy the ice cream. You had told me you liked ice cream," the Mystic said with a smile.

"If your perspective is that you need to eat in order to sustain your body so that you can have a healthy, productive life, then the eating is good and the pleasure that comes with the eating is good. If the focus, however, is on how to trick up the food with wonderful methods of cooking, preparation, serving, eating in special clothes, or eating while listening to special music, then you know that the tail is wagging the dog and not the dog wagging the tail.

"At the other end of the spectrum, there are the sick and unhappy people who make pleasure their primary goal, and whether this is pleasure in the area of food, leading to obesity, or drink, leading to alcoholism, or drugs, leading to enslavement or death, the problem is that the focus is on the gratification rather than the need." The Mystic pulled

Jerry's arm back, forcing him to stop as he gently turned to face him.

Almost as though he knew what was going to happen later that year when the property market collapsed, he looked at Jerry with a penetrating, warm gaze and said:

"You're able to stand alone now, Jerry. You do not need to lean on me or anyone else. Do you remember how we defined leaning?"

"Of course."

"You now have all four keys. You now know that there are no accidents and that everything happens for a purpose. You know that whenever that purpose manifests itself to you as a negative, you know that it is really a gift to you to be changed and developed into a positive. This equipment allows you to be happy, whether or not you have one, two, or three of the blessings at a time, as you know that your internal perspective is independent of the events happening to you, and finally, today you are armed with the shield that chasing after pleasure is an empty vanity at worst and a distraction at best."

Had Jerry known that that was the last time he

would ever see the Mystic, he would never have let him go. He would have sat with him and walked with him through that night into the next day and into the next week and month. As it was, however, Jerry drove the Mystic home, something he had begun to do only in the last year, and paid little attention to their routine goodbyes as he let him out of the car. When he learned the next day that Kaye had died in his sleep from a heart attack at the age of eighty-four, Jerry sobbed for days.

Chapter 24

How Jerry wished he could actually have access to Kaye now.

The morning of the fifth day was bright with sunshine flooding into the room. The birds, some of which Jerry had now learned to identify individually, were hopping from branch to branch in the tree outside. Thomson was coming with his entourage at ten o'clock or thereabouts to pronounce the results of the pathology. Rafaela was sitting patiently in the visitor's chair on the side of the bed, her face drawn. The children were on their way into the hospital, insistent on being present. Jerry did not have the heart to ask the children to stay away, understanding their need for inclusion.

He had spent the last hour talking to Rafaela and explained to her that he had finally learned the secret of how to die.

The secret of how to die came, as everything else he had ever understood in life, from the Mystic and the four keys. Everything was purposeful, and every descent was for the purpose of ascent. Because of this, one could be happy all the time, and seeking pleasure was only a by-product of the way one lived. All of this being true, the important last step was to understand that it is *life* that is important. Life is what needs to be lived, not death. The important thing to learn about dying is to absolutely ignore it. The important thing about living was to live every single minute in case it may be the last. The important thing about living is to understand that each moment is a precious gift, and even those things that appear negative are in themselves precious gifts providing the raw material of one's subsequent action. There can be no action when dead. The way therefore to prepare for death was to keep living. The cancer was purposeful and for the good, however Jerry may have been troubled by it. It allowed him to realize how precious each minute was and how much there was to do and achieve, particularly for others.

So it was when, after the children had arrived and the door opened to admit the white-coated band of doctors with their papers, that Jerry cherished and loved being alive, knowing that whatever was to happen to him, he would relish and value every individual moment left to him as a gift to help others. He was going, he decided, to teach the Mystic's lessons to anyone who would listen.